ENGLISH COTTAGES

JOHN CURTIS

Text by Richard Ashby

SALMON

INTRODUCTION

The simple cottages of England, which we so admire today, often began life as the homes of the more prosperous yeoman farmers. The rural poor lived in huts; it was those who prospered from agriculture who could afford to build more permanent homes. Where timber was plentiful it was used to make the frame of the house and, beginning with the simple 'cruck' frame, techniques became more elaborate allowing the building of more substantial dwellings. Each area had its own style and the timber framing was covered in a variety of materials according to the local tradition, availability, and the wealth of the owner. Where timber was in short supply or where prosperity continued to increase, stone and later brick was used instead. Life in the cottage was hard and amenities few, but by the 18th century the 'Romantic' movement and the cult of the 'picturesque' had invested these simple houses with a desirability which the more leisured classes found attractive. They seemed to embody an ideal of simple living in an increasingly complex world. The Industrial Revolution and the decline in agricultural prosperity depopulated the countryside, but by the end of the 19th century the middle classes were often moving to the villages and establishing a level of comfort in the cottage not seen before. Today, more and more people are returning to the country and the cottage is again a home for those who live and increasingly work there.

Welford-on-Avon, *Warwickshire*

DIDBROOK, *Gloucestershire*

Cruck-framed cottages are a link to the Saxon past, but the simple technique is still in use today. The roof is carried down to the ground by pairs of timbers . The distance between these pairs, a bay, was wide enough for stabling two pairs of oxen and became a standard measurement. Extra bays could be easily added as necessary.

BLANCHLAND, *Northumberland*

The hard weather of the northern counties is matched by the hard stone of the buildings and indeed the hardiness of the folk who live in them. In this isolated north Pennines village the sturdy stone walls and roofs and small windows are designed to keep the elements at bay.

EXTON, *Rutland*

A great belt of limestone sweeps across the centre of England from Dorset to the Lincolnshire Wolds. It varies in colour from rich cream to brown and links this formerly one-roomed simple agricultural labourer's cottage in Rutland with the great terraces and grand houses of Bath.

BIBURY, *Gloucestershire*

Bibury is one of the most beautiful villages in England and its architecture is particularly harmonious. This much photographed row of Cotswold stone cottages began life in the 14th century as a store for wool and was later converted into weavers' cottages in the 17th century.

MILTON ABBAS, *Dorset*

Some landowners thought a cottage or two added a touch of the 'picturesque' to the scene. Others, such as the first Earl of Dorchester, thought they spoiled the view. When having his park designed by the great 'Capability' Brown, he ordered that the village should be moved away. The replacement he provided was itself 'picturesque', though the cottages were still relatively overcrowded by modern standards.

BLAISE HAMLET, *Bristol*

In 1810 Bristol banker John Harford, a Quaker, commissioned the architect, John Nash, to build a model village for the retired servants from his estate at Blaise. The resulting nine cottages are grouped around a green, in the centre of which is a tall sundial with a pump. The village is a rather self-conscious exercise in the 'picturesque'. No two houses are the same and some are thatched and others tiled. Almost all have extraordinarily tall brick chimneys. No doubt it was much admired by Hartford's well-heeled visitors and Blaise was very influential, both in encouraging better housing for estate workers, and in establishing the romantic idea of what a cottage should look like. It epitomises the style which became known as 'cottage orné'.

GROOMBRIDGE, *Kent*

In the south-eastern counties of Kent, Sussex and Surrey there is a lack of good building stone. However the weald of Kent and Sussex was heavily wooded. The area was also a source of good clay for brick and tile making. These 18th century houses make use of these easily available materials. They have a light but sturdy oak timber frame hung with clay tiles and there is weather-boarding too. The bay windows are supported by brick plinths and the roofs are also tiled. Tile hanging is rare outside this area but within it there is a great variety of patterns and tile designs, some imitating brick from a time when brick was taxed.

CAVENDISH, *Suffolk*

These simple thatched and colour-washed cottages date from the 14th century and are known as 'Hyde Park Corner Cottages'. Overlooked by the tower of St. Mary's Church they are now almshouses. The pink wash was originally made from mixing pigs' blood with whitewash and is characteristic of the area, as are the deep thatched roofs with the first floor windows inset.

CLIFTON HAMPDEN, *Oxfordshire*
A number of materials were used to fill the
space between timber frames. In Oxfordshire,
and other areas where clay was plentiful,
brick became popular, especially as it was
more resistant to fire than the earlier wattle
and daub. Nevertheless, many cottages still
kept their thatched roofs.

ALLERFORD, *Somerset*
These sandstone-built cottages, nestling by
a medieval pack-horse bridge, were originally
thatched. The replacement pantiles were
originally imported through Bridgwater, but
were later made in that Somerset port. The
unusual round chimney is a characteristic
of this part of north Somerset.

NORTH BOVEY, *Devon*

This lovely unspoiled village lies on the east side of Dartmoor. Built of the local hard stone which has been whitewashed, the cottages are still thatched in the traditional manner. However, the picture-postcard look of today belies the harshness of life in such places until comparatively recently. The village remained isolated until the coming of the railways; almost everything would have had to be produced locally and the inhabitants would have depended on their own labours for much of their food. There was no electricity and no running water, and cooking and heating was by open fires, or a range if you were fortunate. Outside was an earth closet. Modern plumbing and heating, electricity and sanitation help to make these once humble cottages so desirable today and has ensured their survival.

HARTSOP, *Cumbria*

Home was often the place where you worked for your living too; as it is increasingly in villages again today with the development of modern communications. The women of this village spun their wool during the winter. In the spring the buyers for the cloth mills and the knitters would ride around the area and the spun wool was hung over the gallery and exhibited for sale.

NEWICK, *East Sussex*

This cottage, facing the large village green, is typical of this area, on the edge of the Ashdown Forest. The brick for the lower walls, weather-boarding over the timber frame and tiles on the roof are all local materials. The green was once used for the local cattle market.

BREAMORE, *Hampshire*

Even the style of the timber framing varied from place to place. It was sometimes covered with plaster, wood or tiles, or was left exposed and stained to emphasize the pattern. In Hampshire the framing is square and in-filled with the glowing red brick of the area.

SMARDEN, *Kent*

Much of the heavily forested Weald was cut down from the 14th century onward, both for industry and to clear the land for sheep grazing. The area became prosperous and substantial wood-framed and clad houses were built by those who reaped the benefit of the new industries and commerce. As times changed and prosperity moved elsewhere these houses frequently fell on hard times and were often divided into two or more dwellings for several families, the owners not having the resources to replace the weather-boarding by tile or brick. The larger house shown here once belonged to the church, a major beneficiary of the prosperity brought by wool, and was lived in by three priests who served the local church. It is known as 'The Brothers'.

WYLYE, *Wiltshire*

Chalk downland is a poor place for building stone. Because of the distance it had to be transported stone was expensive. A cheaper substitute was at hand in the profusion of hard flints to be found amongst the chalk. Mixed with mortar it made a good building material. Stone (or brick) was still used for corners. Here it is used in a decorative chequer-board pattern with the flint.

ROXTON, *Bedfordshire*

By the 18th century the search for the picturesque was in full swing and this was reflected in the great remodelling of gardens and parks. Many of these were enhanced by classical temples and other buildings, but as the century developed so a cottage might also be added. At Roxton House a pretty thatched lodge welcomed visitors.

VERYAN, *Cornwall*

The earliest houses of the rural poor were usually round, perhaps in imitation of the tents of mankind's nomadic forebears, and were made of 'cob', a mixture of mud and straw, which was easily obtainable and cheap. The roof was always thatched. It was the yeoman classes, who began to build in timber and then brick or stone, who created the cottages we so admire today. With the development of a variety of building techniques, rectangular buildings became the norm and round buildings became very unusual, largely limited to buildings which had the nature of 'follies'. These two thatched cottages greet visitors to the pretty Cornish village of Veryan. They were built in the early 19th century with no corners, it is said, so that the devil had nowhere to hide!

HIGHER BOCKHAMPTON, *Dorset*

The great English writer, Thomas Hardy, was born in 1840 in this cottage which his great-grandfather had built in 1801. Originally constructed of cob which was susceptible to the rain, it was later faced with brick. Thomas Hardy wrote *Far from the Madding Crowd* here and he describes the cottage in *Under the Greenwood Tree*.

BOVINGTON, *Dorset*

When T E Lawrence wanted to shake off his image as 'Lawrence of Arabia' and to write, he enlisted anonymously in the Tank Corps at Bovington Camp and worked at his writing in this little woodman's cottage, 'Clouds Hill', not far away. The last of its kind, it undoubtedly would have been swept away if it were not for the Lawrence connection.

WYLAM, *Northumberland*

In front of this stone tenement, known as High Street House, ran the Wylam wagonway on which the young George Stevenson would have seen the chaldron wagons loaded with coal, pulled by horses, and early experiments with steam locomotives. He was born here in 1781, only some twenty years after the cottage was built. Four families lived in the house and the Stephensons lived together in one room, no doubt all that could be afforded by his colliery-fireman father. George Stephenson became known as the 'Father of the Railway' and the system to which he gave birth threw off a branch from Kendal to Windermere which William Wordsworth opposed with all his might. He lost this battle but plans for an extension past Dove Cottage to Grasmere and Keswick were dropped.

GRASMERE, *Cumbria*

Dove Cottage, built in 1617 and originally an inn known as 'The Dove and Olive Branch', has achieved worldwide fame as the first permanent home of the poet William Wordsworth and his sister Dorothy, who lived here from 1799 to 1808. It has only been known by its present name since 1890 when the cottage came into the possession of the Wordsworth Trust and opened to the public.

STOURHEAD, *Wiltshire*

The classical buildings which dot this perfect English landscape enhance its magical atmosphere. This cottage probably dates from the laying out of the garden in the mid-18th century, but it was not given its Gothic features until 1806, by which time the style had become quite fashionable before its more scholarly revival later in the century.

BADMINTON, *Gloucestershire*

This cottage, unusually disguised as a castle, was designed by the astronomer Thomas Wright from County Durham whose new theory of the universe made him famous. Wright was also interested in garden design and architecture (he designed pinnacles for Durham Cathedral) and often designed estate buildings for his patrons.

LOWSONFORD, *Warwickshire*

The architecture of the transport revolution was often grand and imposing; the houses provided for the workers, though, were usually much more modest. The design of the canal cottages on the southern part of the Stratford-upon-Avon Canal is particularly unusual. It has been suggested that they were built this way by the navvies and that barrel roofs were the only form they knew having built numerous canal bridges.

THAXTED, *Essex*

These two contrasting buildings stand beside the parish church in this famous small town whose name means 'a place where thatch comes from'. The thatched cottage was once a priest's house and later became an almshouse for four poor people of the parish. Its low, overhanging and heavy-thatched roof and small windows suggest a building that is turning away from the world, perhaps appropriate for a parish priest. It was uninhabitable by the early 20th century and was bought by the church and turned into one dwelling. The other building was built as an almshouse around 1714 and once housed 16 people. It is quite a contrast, the tall chimneys, decorated barge-boards and large windows suggest a certain playfulness and a lightness of spirit. It was renovated in 1975.

LOWER BROADHEATH,
Worcestershire

Brick was used by the Romans but it did not come back into general use until after the Great Fire of London in 1666 when its fire resistance made it much more popular. There had always been brickmaking where local clay was plentiful and of the right quality, and brick was often used to in-fill timber-framed buildings, but it was the development of industrial scale production and the improvements in communications brought by the canals and then the railways which led to its use spreading across the country. It is now the most popular of all house building materials. In this sturdy 19th century cottage, typical of the area, was born England's greatest composer, Sir Edward Elgar. It now belongs to the Elgar Birthplace Trust.

EYAM, *Derbyshire*

In 1665 some 267 out of a total of 350 inhabitants of this Derbyshire village died of the plague. The village went into voluntary isolation after the infection arrived in a box of clothes, and by their selfless actions the villagers prevented the plague from spreading to neighbouring villages, but at the price of their own lives. On many of the cottages are plaques recording the part played in this heroism by the inhabitants.

RUNSWICK BAY, *North Yorkshire*

The unstable cliffs brought destruction here in 1682 when the whole village was swept away by a landslide, leaving just one cottage. Life has always been hard for those making a living from the sea, but today the village, with its steep lanes and colourful houses, is both a tourist attraction and a delightful place to live.

Published in Great Britain by J. Salmon Ltd., Sevenoaks, Kent TN13 1BB. Telephone 01732 452381. Email enquiries@jsalmon.co.uk.
Design by John Curtis. Text and photographs © John Curtis. All rights reserved. No part of this book may be produced, stored in a retrieval system or transmitted in any form or by any means without prior written permission of the publishers.
ISBN 1-84640-035-X Printed in Slovenia © 2006

Title page photograph: Abbots Morton, *Worcestershire*
Front cover photograph: Exton, *Rutland*. Back cover photograph: Portquin, *Cornwall*